Protecting the
# OCEANS

# WHY ARE OCEANS
# IMPORTANT?

By Natalie Hyde

CRABTREE
PUBLISHING COMPANY
WWW.CRABTREEBOOKS.COM

# CRABTREE
## PUBLISHING COMPANY
### WWW.CRABTREEBOOKS.COM

**Author:** Natalie Hyde

**Editorial director:** Kathy Middleton

**Editor:** Janine Deschenes

**Proofreader:** Wendy Scavuzzo

**Design:** Margaret Salter

**Production coordinator
  and Prepress technician:**
  Margaret Salter

**Print coordinator:** Katherine Berti

**Photo Credits:**
b=Bottom, t=Top, tr=Top Right, tl=Top Left

Shutterstock: Emil Litov, title page;
Sopotnicki, p4 (b); Sandro Pavlov, p6 (b);
Edgloris Marys, p28 (b)

Wikimedia Commons: Creative Commons, p20 (b);

All other images from Shutterstock

**Library and Archives Canada Cataloguing in Publication**

Title: Why are oceans important? / Natalie Hyde.
Names: Hyde, Natalie, 1963-
Description: Series statement: Protecting the oceans |
  Includes bibliographical references and  index.
Identifiers: Canadiana (print) 20200283812 |
  Canadiana (ebook) 20200283820 |
  ISBN 9780778782049 (hardcover) |
  ISBN 9780778782087 (softcover) |
  ISBN 9781427126085 (HTML)
Subjects: LCSH: Ocean—Juvenile literature. |
  LCSH: Marine ecology—Juvenile literature. |
  LCSH: Nature—Effect of human beings on—Juvenile literature.
Classification: LCC GC21.5 .H93 2020 | DDC j551.46—dc23

**Library of Congress Cataloging-in-Publication Data**

Names: Hyde, Natalie, 1963- author.
Title: Why are oceans important? / Natalie Hyde.
Description: New York : Crabtree Publishing Company, 2021. |
  Series: Protecting the oceans | Includes index.
Identifiers: LCCN 2020029732 (print) | LCCN 2020029733 (ebook) |
  ISBN 9780778782049 (hardcover) |
  ISBN 9780778782087 (paperback) |
  ISBN 9781427126085 (ebook)
Subjects: LCSH: Ocean--Juvenile literature.
Classification: LCC QL122.2 .H93 2021  (print) |
  LCC QL122.2  (ebook) | DDC  591.77--dc23
LC record available at https://lccn.loc.gov/2020029732
LC ebook record available at https://lccn.loc.gov/2020029733

**Crabtree Publishing Company**
www.crabtreebooks.com          1-800-387-7650

Printed in the U.S.A./082020/CG20200710

**Published in Canada**
**Crabtree Publishing**
616 Welland Ave.
St. Catharines, Ontario
L2M 5V6

**Published in the United States**
**Crabtree Publishing**
347 Fifth Ave
Suite 1402-145
New York, NY 10016

**Published in the United Kingdom**
**Crabtree Publishing**
Maritime House
Basin Road North, Hove
BN41 1WR

**Published in Australia**
**Crabtree Publishing**
3 Charles Street
Coburg North
VIC, 3058

# CONTENTS

Depending on Oceans . . . . . . . . . . . . . 4

Diverse Ocean Life . . . . . . . . . . . . . . . 6

Get to Know the Oceans . . . . . . . . . . . 8

Living in the Oceans . . . . . . . . . . . . . . 10

Plants in the Oceans . . . . . . . . . . . . . . 12

Why Are Oceans Important to Us? . . . . 14

Climate Buffer . . . . . . . . . . . . . . . . . . 16

The Fishing Industry . . . . . . . . . . . . . . 18

Natural Resources and Power . . . . . . . . 20

Tourism and Recreation . . . . . . . . . . . . 22

Transportation . . . . . . . . . . . . . . . . . . 24

Oceans in Danger . . . . . . . . . . . . . . . . 26

Taking Ocean Action . . . . . . . . . . . . . . 28

Glossary . . . . . . . . . . . . . . . . . . . . . . . 30

Learning More . . . . . . . . . . . . . . . . . . . 31

Index and About the Author . . . . . . . . . 32

# DEPENDING ON OCEANS

The town of Witless Bay, Newfoundland and Labrador, has always relied on the sea. It was founded as a fishing village. Cod fishing was used for food and for trade. In 1992, the cod fishery was closed because fish stocks were so low. The town turned to tourism to boost its **economy**. Visitors could take tours to see puffins and whales, including humpback whales. The town rebounded. But these waters are within major shipping routes. The routes allow ships to bring in much-needed supplies and take out products for trade. However, the noise and pollution from ships disturb the behavior of the whales and sea birds, which is a threat to marine tours.

HALE WATCH

Gaffer VI

**40%** of the world's population lives within 62 miles (100 km) of the coast.

## Vital in Every Way

People need the oceans. They provide us with food, jobs, recreation, and transportation. The seafloor is also a source of metals and **minerals**. Some communities around the world rely on the ocean for living space. Halong Bay in Vietnam, for example, is home to four floating villages. Floating buildings and docks allow the people to work close to the fish and pearl farms that they harvest. Oceans also provide power through tidal and offshore wind farms.

Oceans also affect the climate and weather around the world. Ocean currents help move warm and cold air around the globe, keeping temperatures from becoming super hot at the equator and frigid by the poles. This movement of warm and cold water creates weather patterns such as wind and rain on land.

The Halong Bay floating villages are also tourism hotspots, bringing money to the people who live there.

# DIVERSE OCEAN LIFE

**Humans are not the only living things to depend on oceans. Millions of plants and animals need it to survive.**

Some marine plants live in shallower water and along shorelines. Seagrass, seaweed, and mangrove trees provide food and shelter for **marine life**. Kelp are the largest sea plants, creating forests underwater. The tiniest plants are called phytoplankton. They are a marine algae made up of only one cell. They float in the ocean taking in carbon dioxide and using the Sun to make oxygen. These tiny plants provide most of the oxygen on Earth.

Giant kelp grows extremely quickly—11 to 12 inches (28–30cm) per day! It is a habitat for many living things, such as fish and squid.

## OCEAN ACTION

## Jean-Michel Cousteau

Jean-Michel Cousteau is the son of famous ocean explorer Jacques Cousteau. Jean-Michel founded the Ocean Futures Society in 1999. Its mission is to explore our global ocean. It hopes to inspire and educate people worldwide to act responsibly to protect oceans. Through its work, the society wants to recognize the ocean's vital importance to the survival of all life on Earth.

An estimated 50 to 80 percent of all life on Earth is found in the oceans.

## Massive Mammals

Ocean creatures range from coral, which are **microscopic** creatures that make up coral reefs, to the largest mammal on Earth: the blue whale. Marine animals live in all areas of the ocean. They range from dolphins that spend most of their time on the surface, to the mid-ocean jellyfish, to sea spiders that live on the ocean floor. Some, such as the narwhal, live in cold arctic waters. Others, such as seahorses, live in warm tropical seas.

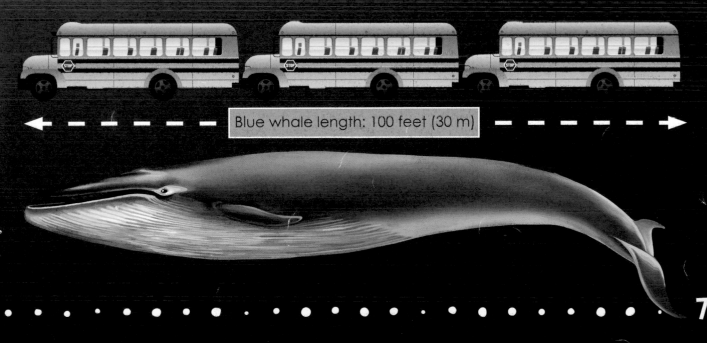

STOP    STOP    STOP

◄ – – – – – – – – – – – Blue whale length: 100 feet (30 m) – – – – – – – – – – – ►

# GET TO KNOW THE OCEANS

We divide the world's ocean waters into five oceans. They are, from largest to smallest; the Pacific, Atlantic, Indian, Southern, and Arctic Oceans.

The five oceans are not separate like lakes. They are connected and the water flows from one ocean to another. All of the ocean waters together are called the World Ocean. It covers more than 70 percent of Earth's surface.

The Pacific Ocean is larger than all of Earth's land combined.

**Atlantic Ocean**

**Pacific Ocean**

The Atlantic Ocean has a powerful current that flows north from Mexico up the coast as far as Newfoundland. This current, called the Gulf Stream, brings warm water that affects the climate of the east coast of North America. It is also the reason palm trees grow in the very south of England.

The Arctic Ocean is partly covered by sea ice throughout the year, and almost completely covered in winter months. However, as ocean temperatures increase due to **global warming**, the sea ice is melting and less of the ocean is covered. The Arctic has large continental shelves, or shallow seabeds, that hold oil and gas **reserves**.

**Arctic Ocean**

Early civilizations used the Indian Ocean for trade and travel. Near the coasts, there is a large continental shelf. The shelf contains plenty of fish to feed the roughly two billion people who live along its shores.

**Pacific Ocean**

The Mariana Trench, north of Papua New Guinea, is the lowest point on Earth. The Pacific is also home to the Great Barrier Reef off the coast of Australia.

**Indian Ocean**

**Southern Ocean**

The Southern Ocean is also known as the Antarctic Ocean. The Antarctic Circumpolar Current creates strong winds and waves. This ocean has unique marine animals such as ice fish and the warty squid.

# LIVING IN THE OCEANS

Oceans may look empty, but they are full of life. Diverse marine life includes microscopic plants and animals that feed larger fish, mammals, and birds. Scientists say there are up to one million different species of animals in the ocean.

Life in the oceans creates **food chains**. Tiny algae are eaten by tiny shrimp-like creatures. These are eaten by small fish such as sunfish. Small fish are eaten by bigger creatures such as squid. Squid are a favorite food of larger fish such as tuna. Tuna are prey to sharks such as the tiger shark or great white.

Coral and sponges that grow on the seafloor look like plants, but they are actually animals. As adults, they do not move but grow in colonies, or groups, to create reefs. Both corals and sponges grow slowly and provide structure for many other kinds of sea life such as clown fish and rockfish.

Humans learn a lot from ocean plant and animal adaptations. Glow-in-the-dark products, for example, are inspired by bioluminescence.

## Inspiring Adaptations

Creatures have **adapted** to living in all areas of oceans: shallow warm water, cold arctic water, and under crushing pressure at the ocean floor. In the darkness, some creatures communicate using light. This is called bioluminescence. These creatures create light using only chemicals in their bodies. Humans can learn from the way these creatures thrive in these environments. Ocean adaptations give us insights on how we can also adapt or build structures using their techniques. We are still discovering new life forms in the oceans all the time. Scientists have explored just five percent of the world's oceans. This means there are many, many ocean life forms left to discover.

# 95%
of the world's oceans have not yet been explored.

# PLANTS IN THE OCEANS

Oceans are home to many different kinds of plants. Plants range from tiny algae to large mangrove trees. They are found at all levels in the ocean. Some float near the surface. Others anchor themselves to the seafloor.

Seagrass and seaweeds have roots that cling to the seafloor. They are usually found in shallow ocean waters near coastlines where they can still get sunlight. Seagrass is food for many kinds of marine creatures such as green turtles, manatees, and crabs. It also shelters juvenile, or young, fish until they are large enough to survive in the open ocean.

1 acre (1/2 hectare) of seagrass can support

Similar to how mowing a lawn keeps grass healthy, green turtles improve seagrass beds by trimming the grass as they eat.

# Jean Wiener

Jean Wiener was born in Haiti. Growing up, he saw how important the environment was, especially along the coast and in the sea. After becoming a marine biologist, he founded the Fondation pour la Protection de la Biodiversité Marine (FoProBiM) in Haiti in 1992. It is a nonprofit organization dedicated to saving mangrove trees and coral reefs, and to cleaning the island nation's beaches. Thanks to Wiener's and FoProBiM's work, in 2013, the Haitian government signed the nation's first **Marine Protected Areas** into law.

**50 million invertebrates**

**=**

**40,000 fish**

## All-Purpose Plants

Kelp is a type of seaweed that is shelter for sea creatures, but is also harvested by humans. Its **cell walls** have a gel-like substance that is used to thicken ice cream, jelly, and toothpaste. Seaweeds are also dried and eaten around the world, or put on poor soil as fertilizer. Mangroves are forests of trees that grow in shallow salty water along coasts. Their roots help prevent soil erosion from winds, waves, and floods.

# WHY ARE OCEANS IMPORTANT TO US?

**Humans have always been connected to oceans. They provide everything we need to live: oxygen, water, food, transportation, and power.**

70%

of our oxygen ($O_2$) comes from the ocean.

Oxygen is necessary for life. Without it, the Earth would be a barren rock in space. As plants make food from sunlight, they give off oxygen. This is what creates the air that supports life. We breathe oxygen every day. The majority of the oxygen we breathe comes from ocean plants.

**25%**

of human-made carbon dioxide ($CO_2$) is absorbed by marine plants.

$CO_2$

## Slowing Climate Change

Healthy oceans need to have a lot of marine plants. To create oxygen during **photosynthesis**, the plants take in the gas carbon dioxide from the air. Carbon dioxide is called a **greenhouse gas** because it traps heat in the atmosphere, warming the temperature of Earth. By taking carbon dioxide out of the air, ocean plants help to reduce greenhouse gases and slow **climate change**. Many of these marine plants are microscopic. Because we can't easily see them, we do not always realize the important role they play or notice when their numbers are decreasing. Preventing pollution and chemical runoff that can harm these ocean plants is vital to our own survival.

# CLIMATE BUFFER

**More of Earth's surface is covered with water than with land. That huge amount of water stores heat and carbon dioxide—and is responsible for climate and weather patterns.**

Oceans hold more heat in the top 10 feet (3 m) of their water than the entire atmosphere. Heat is absorbed during the day and released at night, keeping temperatures near the coast more constant. By holding and moving huge amounts of warm and cold water, oceans help seasons to change slowly. Without ocean currents, temperatures on Earth would be more extreme: much hotter at the equator and much colder at the poles. This would mean less of our planet's land would be habitable.

Oceans regulate seasonal temperatures, helping animals and plants gradually adapt to rising or falling temperatures.

Cold water current

Warm water current

Scientists studying the effects climate change has on currents have found that the Atlantic current may be slowing down. This could cause more extreme weather.

# Weather and Currents

Currents move warm and cold water around the globe. This movement creates winds, rain, snow, and storms. Hurricanes, cyclones, and typhoons all form over water. Winds then often push these storms over land. Climate change is warming our oceans. This is changing weather patterns around the world.

The number of summer days with extreme heat in Europe has tripled since 1950. This also means we are seeing more frequent and more powerful storms. The number of tropical storms in the North Atlantic has increased more than 40% since the 1950s. Scientists say if our oceans keep warming, storms will likely become even more powerful.

# THE FISHING INDUSTRY

Fishing and the production of seafood provides livelihoods and food sources for millions of people. Around the world, about 200 million people have jobs in the fishing industry. They provide the 170 million tons (154 million metric tons) of seafood eaten by humans each year.

The fishing industry is important in Myanmar. This fisherman catches fish for food.

Seafood eaten by humans includes fish, shellfish, seaweed, and fish used for fish oil. The amount of seafood people around the globe eat has doubled in the past 50 years. Fish is high in protein and low in fat. Oily fish contain nutrients and certain types of **fatty acids** that are good for our health. Fish can also be less expensive than other types of protein. This means people in poorer areas of the world can still have a healthy diet.

## OCEAN ACTION

## Nina Jensen

Nina Jensen is the CEO of REV Ocean, a nonprofit company whose goal is to make oceans healthy again. The company is building the world's largest research and expedition vessel. It will be able to host 60 researchers at any time. It hopes the research will find solutions for the ocean's problems.

## Ocean Livelihoods

Jobs in the seafood and fishing industry include people who fish, boat builders, fish processing plant workers, market sellers, and dockworkers. Aquaculture is also known as fish farming. Fish and other seafood are raised in netted or fenced areas of water. Salmon, halibut, oysters, and clams can all be farmed. Today, about half of all the seafood produced for humans to eat comes from aquaculture.

Seaweed is also farmed for food and other uses.

## Medicine

Some marine creatures are becoming important in the treatment of human diseases. A kind of bacteria from the seafloor is being tested as a new treatment for certain kinds of cancer. The skin of a fish called tilapia is often used to treat burns.

Global fish production in 2019

196 million tons (178 million metric tons)

26 Great Pyramids of Giza

# NATURAL RESOURCES AND POWER

To reduce climate change, the world is looking for ways to produce power without using fossil fuels. Part of the solution can be found in our oceans. Oceans can help produce renewable energy **with both tidal power stations and wind power stations.**

One benefit of tidal power is that tides are **predictable**. They rely on the pull of the moon and, unlike solar power, tides are not affected by clouds. The power of the water moving in and out with the tide turns **turbines**, which creates electricity. There are eight tidal power stations around the world with at least 10 more stations being planned.

There are many wind turbines on land around the world. Wind turbines set up in the ocean provide more power because the winds are not slowed down by buildings and mountains like they are on land. The Beatrice Offshore Wind Farm off the shore in the north of Scotland opened in 2019. It can generate enough power for 450,000 homes.

The Annapolis Royal Generating Station is a tidal station in the Bay of Fundy in Nova Scotia, Canada. It generates enough power for 4,500 homes.

Scientists estimate that there is enough gold in the ocean floor to give each person on Earth 9 pounds (4 kg)!

**LB** 0.45 kg

**LB** 0.45 kg

**LB** 0.45 kg

**LB** 0.45 kg

**LB** 0.45 kg

**LB** 0.45 kg

**LB** 0.45 kg

**LB** 0.45 kg

**LB** 0.45 kg

There are more than 1,500 offshore oil rigs around the world.

## Marine Mining

The ocean floor also contains valuable resources. Sand and gravel are mined from the ocean floor for construction. There are also precious metals and gems such as gold, silver, copper, nickel, cobalt, and diamonds on the seafloor. Scientists estimate that there could be trillions of dollars worth of gold in the ocean. Oil and gas are also valuable resources in the ocean.

# TOURISM AND RECREATION

Oceans are also important for people as a place for recreation, adventure, and travel. Coastal areas around the world depend on the tourism industry.

Water sports such as water-skiing, sailing, diving, and surfing are popular around the world. The ASP (Association of Surfing Professionals) World Tour, for example, is a series of surfing competitions at different sites to find the world champion.

Divers explore reefs and shipwrecks. Some even look for treasure from sunken ships. Millions of people also enjoy relaxing on beaches and swimming to cool off. Oceans give us the opportunity for enjoyment and exercise.

Sport fishing is a favorite pastime for millions of people. People who do deep-sea sport fishing try to catch tuna, sharks, and marlin. Many people participate in offshore fishing competitions—sometimes for prizes of more than $1million!

# Hanli Prinsloo

South African Hanli Prinsloo is the founder and CEO of the oceans conservation trust called "I Am Water". Her team connects diverse communities to the oceans to discover life beneath the waves first hand. Young people from **underprivileged** communities along the coasts are invited to explore the mystery and beauty of the ocean. This way, Hanli hopes to encourage them to appreciate and want to protect our oceans.

## The Tourism Industry

Cruise ships are a type of luxury travel. Huge ocean ships take tourists across the sea to visit countries around the globe. Each year more than 20 million passengers explore the world by cruise ship. These trips help bring **remote** areas much needed money from tourism. This money helps create and run protected natural areas and historic sites, such as the unique creatures of the Galapagos Islands.

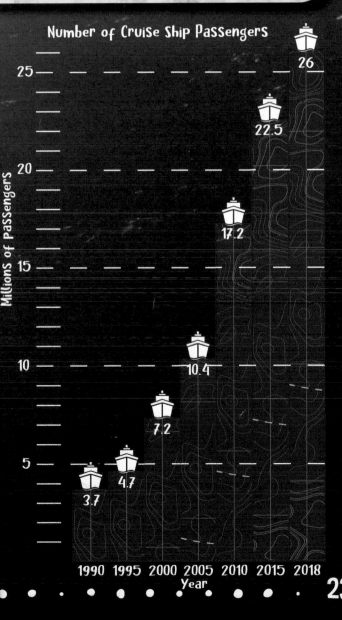

**Number of Cruise Ship Passengers**

Millions of Passengers

25 —
20 —
15 —
10 —
5 —

26
22.5
17.2
10.4
7.2
4.7
3.7

1990  1995  2000  2005  2010  2015  2018
Year

# TRANSPORTATION

People have used oceans and other waterways to get around since ancient times. It was often much easier than trying to go overland. As ships became bigger and sailing improved, people began to explore farther and immigrate to new countries.

Shipping means moving cargo between **seaports**. All kinds and sizes of ships move every kind of product imaginable: food, clothing, cars, chemicals, oil, animals. Shipping is the least expensive way to move large amounts over long distances. 90 percent of trade around the world is done by ship. There are around 50,000 container ships operating in the oceans. Because of storms or rough seas, hundreds of these containers fall off these ships each year.

The largest modern container ships can carry more than 12,000 40-foot (12-meter) containers!

## Traveling by Ship

Oceans are transportation routes for people, too. While traveling by ship is not as popular as travelling by plane, some people prefer the slower pace and life at sea. Travel by ship is also more environmentally friendly than travel by plane. The Queen Mary 2 is an ocean liner that makes regular trips across the Atlantic Ocean from New York City, New York, to Southampton, England. The trip takes seven days. Ferries cross shorter stretches of the ocean where there are no bridges or tunnels. They make regular crossings on a schedule, and carry people, vehicles, and small amounts of cargo.

**One Shipping container can hold...**

48,000 bananas   OR   12,000 Shoeboxes   OR 24,900 tin cans

# OCEANS IN DANGER

We use and rely on oceans in many parts of our lives. But we do not always take good care of this valuable and important resource. Some of our activities are endangering the world's oceans.

Pollution from shipping, recreation, oil spills, and poor management of our garbage has led to problems with water quality and the health of marine life. Plastic is flowing down rivers into the oceans. The Sun and waves begin to break it down into tiny pieces. These pieces are accidentally swallowed by fish and can eventually kill them. Allowing tons of plastic to end up in the oceans is a threat to our food supply from the ocean.

**1,000** Per year

**1** million per year

Animals killed by ocean plastic

In addition to clouding the water, mining can also put toxic metals into the oceans and into our food chain.

## Pollution Problems

Oil spills from container ships or oil platforms poison the water, **suffocate** fish, and coat sea bird feathers so they can't fly. Noise pollution from heavy ocean traffic disrupts communication between marine animals such as whales. They have trouble finding food, their families, and their migration routes.

**Dredging** from mining damages seafloor habitats. It also brings up tons of sediment that clouds the water. This makes it difficult for marine plants to use the Sun for photosynthesis. This can affect the amount of carbon dioxide that gets taken out of our atmosphere, speeding up climate change. It also decreases the amount of oxygen in our atmosphere.

# TAKING OCEAN ACTION

People around the world are recognizing that our oceans are vital to our lives. Achieving ocean health is one of the Sustainable Development Goals of the United Nations (UN). These goals aim to tackle the most pressing challenges facing Earth, creating a more sustainable world.

World Oceans Day is June 8th. It is meant as a day to honor, help protect, and conserve our oceans. It is also a time to check in to see if plans to decrease damage and pollution and improve the health of our World Ocean are working. Each year, the United Nations selects a different theme. Some past themes include "Our oceans: greening our future" and "Healthy Oceans, Healthy Planet." Different activities in different countries include beach cleanups, art contests, photo competitions, and sustainable seafood events.

Research World Oceans Day activities in your area and join in. Or, create your own activity to raise awareness about protecting the oceans.

In Washington, DC in 2019, Sea Youth Rise Up delegates also organized a park and river cleanup. Volunteers collected 976.5 pounds (443 kg) of debris.

# Leaders of the Future

The World Oceans Day Youth Advisory Council is a network of young leaders. They want to connect and unite youth around the world to help create a better future with healthier oceans. They help develop ideas for World Oceans Day that will get people around the world involved. They believe that by working together, they can combine their strategies and resources to inspire and support youth to protect our oceans.

Sea Youth Rise Up was launched on World Oceans Day in 2016. It is a platform for youth to give them a voice and resources to put their ideas and plans into practice to protect our oceans. In 2019 a youth delegation, or group of representatives, traveled to Washington, DC. They met with politicians and committees to **lobby** new laws over our use of plastics and more funding for the National Oceanic and Atmospheric Administration (NOAA).

# GLOSSARY

**adapted** Made changes to thrive in new conditions

**cell wall** Outer layer that gives a cell support and acts as a filter

**climate change** The change in Earth's climate patterns due to higher levels of carbon dioxide in the atmosphere

**dredging** Scooping out mud with a machine

**economy** The wealth and resources of a country

**fatty acids** Building blocks of fat in our bodies

**food chains** Chains of organisms in which each member uses the member below as food

**global warming** The gradual increase in Earth's temperature, caused in part by human activity

**greenhouse gas** A gas that traps heat in Earth's atmosphere

**invertebrates** Animals with no backbone or inner skeleton

**lobby** To try to influence laws, especially related to politics

**Marine Protected Areas** Areas of ocean protected by government

**microscopic** Very tiny; can only be seen with a microscope

**minerals** Solid natural substances

**photosynthesis** Process by which plants use sunlight to make food

**predictable** Act in a way that is constant and reliable

**remote** Located far away from main populations

**renewable energy** Energy from a source that doesn't run out

**reserves** Supplies of something able to be used in the future

**seaports** Harbors or towns on the coast involved in shipping

**suffocate** Cause to die from lack of oxygen

**sustainable** A resource used without being used up or damaged

**turbines** Machines with rotating parts that provide power

**underprivileged** Not having as much money, education, or things as other people

# LEARNING MORE

## Books

Johnson, Robin. *Oceans Inside Out*. Crabtree Publishing, 2014.

DK. *Ocean!: Our Watery World as You've Never Seen It Before*. DK Children, 2020.

Kalman, Bobbie. *Explore Earth's Five Oceans*. Crabtree Publishing, 2010.

## Websites

**https://www.cbc.ca/kidscbc2/the-feed/world-oceans-quiz**
Take CBC Kid's quiz on the oceans for World Oceans Day.

**https://climatekids.nasa.gov/ocean/**
NASA's Climate Kids explains what is happening in our oceans.

**https://kids.nationalgeographic.com/explore/nature/habitats/ocean/**
View the ocean's amazing animals with National Geographic Kids.

# INDEX

adaptations 11
Antarctic Ocean 9
Arctic Ocean 8, 9
Atlantic Ocean 8–9, 17, 25
Beatrice Offshore Wind Farm 20
bioluminescence 11
carbon dioxide 6, 15, 16, 27
climate change 15, 17, 20, 27
container ships 24, 25
continental shelves 9
coral 7, 10, 13
Cousteau, Jean-Michel 6
cruise ships 23
currents 5, 9, 16, 17, 25
exploring oceans 6, 11, 22, 23
extreme temperatures 16, 17
ferries 25
fish farms 5, 19
fishing, sport 22
fishing industry 4, 9, 18–19
floating villages 5
Fondation pour la Protection de la Biodiversité Marine (FoProBiM) 13
food 4, 5, 9, 14, 18, 19, 26, 28
food chains 10, 27
global warming 9
gold 21
Great Barrier Reef 9
greenhouse gases 15
Gulf Stream 9
Halong Bay, Vietnam 5
I Am Water 23
Indian Ocean 8, 9
Jensen, Nina 19
kelp 6, 13

mangrove trees 6, 12, 13
Mariana Trench 9
marine life 4, 6, 7, 9, 10–11, 12, 18, 26, 27
Marine Protected Areas 13
medicine 19
metals and minerals 5, 21, 27
mining 21, 27
Ocean Futures Society 6
ocean liners 25
oil and gas 9, 21, 27
oxygen production 5, 14, 15
Pacific Ocean 8, 9
phytoplankton 6
plants 6, 10, 12, 13, 14, 15, 16, 27
plastics 26, 29
pollution 4, 15, 26–27, 28–29
power generation 5, 14, 20
pressure 11
Prinsloo, Hanli 23
recreation 5, 22, 23, 25
reefs 7, 9, 10, 13, 22
renewable energy 20
researchers 19
REV Ocean 19

seabirds 4, 10, 27
seafloor/ocean floor 5, 7, 10, 11, 12, 19, 21, 27
seafood 18, 19
seagrass 6, 12
seaweed 6, 12, 13, 18, 19
shipping 4, 24, 25, 26, 27
Southern Ocean 8, 9
temperature regulation 5, 9, 16
tidal power 5, 20
tourism 4, 5, 22, 23
transportation 5, 14, 24, 25
weather patterns 5, 16, 17
whales 4, 7, 27
Wiener, Jean 13
wind farms 5, 20
winds 5, 9, 13, 17, 20
Witless Bay, NL 4
World Oceans Day 28–29
world's oceans 8–9

# ABOUT THE AUTHOR

Natalie Hyde has written more than 90 fiction and non-fiction books for young readers. When she gets time to relax, one of her favorite places is to be beside the ocean on a warm, sandy beach.